Weight of Snow

Also by Jennifer Chrystie and published by Ginninderra Press
Polishing the Silver

Jennifer Chrystie

Weight of Snow

Acknowledgements and Thanks

Some of these poems were first published in
ars poetica, *Blue Dog*, *cordite*, *Earthworks* (Poetica Christi Anthology), *Everyday Splendour* (Poetica Christi anthology), *Famous Reporter*, *foam:e*, *From Here* (Poets@Watsonia anthology), *Going Down Swinging*, *Hecate*, *Hobo*, *Horizons* (Poetica Christi anthology), *Moving Galleries*, *New Beginnings* (Poetica Christi anthology), *page seventeen*, *paper wasp*, *Poetrix*, *Poetry Monash*, *Reflecting on Melbourne* (Poetica Christi Press), *Shot Glass Journal* (US), *Tears in the Fence* (wandering dog website), *the perfect diary*, *Tirra Lirra*.

'The Rajah Quilt' was published in *Best Australian Poems 2012* (Black Inc)

'Everest' won the Poetica Christi Press 2006 Annual Poetry Competition.

Sincere thanks to the Nandina poets for their friendship, advice and encouragement; to The Wordsmiths and Poets@Watsonia; to my husband John for his patience and loving support as always; and to my editor, Stephen Matthews, who has brought this project to fruition.

Weight of Snow
ISBN 978 1 74027 809 6
Copyright © text Jennifer Chrystie 2013
Cover design: Julie Jay

First published 2013
Reprinted 2017

GINNINDERRA PRESS
PO Box 3461 Port Adelaide SA 5015
www.ginninderrapress.com.au

Contents

Foreword	9
Beginning	11
Weight of Snow	12
Everest	13
Purnululu	14
Lookout	15
Tree House	16
Cradle Mountain	17
View	18
Platform	19
Snapshots	20
Stillborn	22
Comet	23
In the year of my birth	24
The Annual Sunday School Picnic at Hanging Rock	26
Man Playing Harmonica	27
Wrist Bones	28
The four of us	29
Travelling Companion	30
Taking Tea	32
Elemental	33
Snow Gum	35
Span	36
Digging	37
My Poem	38
On the balcony	39
Immortality	40
Transience	41
Looking Back	43
Plenty River Trail	44

Haiku	45
City Park	46
Luna Park	47
Angel on Swanston	48
Josephine Bonaparte at Malmaison	49
Marie Curie	50
Einstein's Wife	51
Neptune's Wife	52
Spontaneous Generation	53
To make bread	55
Breakthrough	56
Crane	57
Flamingo	58
Flapper	59
Haiku	60
White Bees	61
Cathedral	62
Wasp Attack	63
Heat Wave	64
Bushfire	66
Burning	67
Waking	68
Waiting for the light	69
Book Launch	70
Lake Bonney	71
Cast	72
Coast	73
A Visit to the Aquarium	74
Perspective	75
Leaving	76
Pluto to Proserpina	77
Underground car park at dawn	78

Burke longs for Julia	79
Aboard The Lady Jocelyn	80
The Rajah Quilt	81
Lady of Sandstone	83
Lady of Limestone	84
Lady of Bluestone	85
Writers' Block	86
Soliloquy	87

Foreword

This is a thoughtful and diverse collection, rich with imagery. Family relationships are viewed from various angles and always with compassion.

'Snapshots' is a telling reminder of the restrictions once imposed by society on women. 'In the year of my birth' evokes a time of war and will strike a chord with many readers. The poet's background in science informs poems such as 'Beginnings' and 'Elemental'. 'Cast' describes a Holocaust Memorial by the Danube, where 'Metal shoes wait/in a higgledy row…' The horror unfolds in four tight stanzas, and is unforgettable. Historical figures are given a voice: 'Josephine Bonaparte', 'Marie Curie' and 'Einstein's Wife' add to our understanding of their lives. 'Burke Longs for Julia' is a poignant but unsentimental look at the vulnerable side of the explorer. 'Wrist Bones' left me with the image of those bones kept in a jar, and the poet's loving observation that although her father could no longer paint oils, it didn't 'stop him/conjuring trinkets from our ears/ with a flick of his wrist.'

Intensely observant and memorable, these poems should find a wide readership.

Lorraine McGuigan, Poetry Monash

Beginning

After *Carbonite*, Howard Arkley, 1973

Dark matter fogged
in cosmic disarray
Pink   green   blue squiggles
morphing letters like F
for failure or perfect pairs
G/C and A/T rungs
of the DNA ladder spiralling
quavering through a stave
of minims

A skewed frame melting
in and out of star stuff
and we in the dark
how and why of it

Weight of Snow

Snow muffles the echo
of currawongs on limbs
rendered anonymous

The slide begins
in crooked lines at first
all my limbs busy with balance

The lake has iced to opacity cracked here
and there glimmers of black
Toes freeze, sweat clouds my eyes

Steepness derails me
bruising on curves and helplessness
harks back to childhood

A tinkle of melt water flutes the track
trees unload their burdens
Each leaf is stencilled on blue

Everest

Black fingers clutch the icy crag
His gloves are shredded, his clothes wet through
He's coming home in a body bag

Down in the valley he made the brag
he'd be the first to see the peak view
Black fingers clutch the icy crag

Halfway up, breathless, he started to lag
his legs ton weights, his face grey-blue
He's coming home in a body bag

When he passed a corpse holding a flag
he realised the damage ego can do
Black fingers clutch the icy crag

They turned up the oxygen, carried his swag
but his speech was slurred. It was then they knew
he'd be coming home in a body bag

The highest mountain, the hardest drag
only existed for him to subdue
Black fingers clutch the icy crag
He's coming home in a body bag

Purnululu

Sky blue/earth orange.
Exhilaration/fear
propel us weak-kneed
to a helicopter churning

We strap in tightly for horror
no doors   You take the front
and at the rear I clutch the metal bar
as if electrocuted

Ascending at speed we veer and tip
over theatres of stone   Giant beehives
striped yellow and black take centre stage
I feel the pull of the ancient land

and my heritage tumbles before my eyes
Layer on layer of mammals   reptiles   frogs
and fish ghost in and out   their fossil forms
rippling down the hot funnel of air

You hold fast to the edge of the seat
the pilot croons his commentary until
like some prehistoric dragonfly
we wheel at last for home

Lookout

Insert compass point and describe an arc
puckered shoreline softened by lips of foam
where waves saunter in with booty
from Antarctica

Up high looking down and out I see
the rocks flattened in grey-brown obeisance
and the sea surrendering Prussian blue
to turquoise

Protean clouds skylark
chase their shadows in a rollicking
game of catch-me-if-you-can
I feel vertigo coming on

My fall would be broken
by scruffy tea tree holding the line
from cliff top to beach where anglers
skirt grey aprons of skates

Sunbathers are nonpareils on sand cake
ignored by wheeling falcons
in their hunt for more docile prey
A black-and-white butterfly plummets and soars

Tree House

A nineteenth-century Barossa Valley family
lived in a hollow tree for two years

Scarred by the rough beat
of heartwood and glued together
by teardrops of sap we hear the wind stir

the leaves with snatches of song drifting
on pollen tides and at night the dreams
of roosting birds mingle with our own

Scents cascade in symphony around us
eucalyptus   wattle   fig   the droppings
from animals dizzy the vegetable soul

A breeze down low is a gale
up high   creaking timbers like an ark
braving its worst waves

Our tree takes life and death in its stride
though it goes nowhere   except up
to the light and down to the dark

Cradle Mountain

The mountain rocks a cradled baby
chest and feet wisped in cloud
or maybe legend got it wrong
and the mountain rocks a dead climber
one every five years

This time we've come prepared
for cold wet weather
Gloves, raincoats, thick boots
So much water yet not enough
for spindly gums dying
for decades

Walkers rub shoulders
with dolerite boulders intruding
into an ancient landscape
sculpted by wind and water
More awesome than Parthenon
or Pyramid

We tread the boardwalk marked
by blocks of wombat dung
cross clear brown streams
trespass on enchanted glades
Moss drips from branches patched
with orange and white lichen

swathes fallen trunks
in the greenest possible farewell
The spirits need to be appeased
They can, like the weather
so easily turn

View

End of the honeymoon
we drive down a straight avenue
the city condensing from fog

Slipping back under the cowl
of carefree habit
is no longer an option

Houses cling to cliffs
a pruned tree grows
new leaves

A sign reads Free Bricks
but they are freer than we are
smooth-mortared together

Turning circles within circles
we take the wrong spoke
drive miles through sage green

backtrack into deepening pink
frail flower of beginnings

Platform

Far from the sea, three gulls
necks S-bent, squabble on the line
Two gang up, turn on the third

Ruffled squawks fly
as the hiss of heavy brakes
bears down

Alighting from the train, three women
in loose tangle unravelling
One woman straggles

Glaring at her, the other two hiss
a gaggle of foreign exchange
a strange and shocking sibilance

All three move as if side-stepping
snakes and vanish up the escalator
trailing skeins of hate

Snapshots

Niagara Falls...1913

The moon wilts in a pale sky
Arcs of spray splinter light
A serious three-year-old girl sits rigid
between stern parents who had wanted to travel
childless through a tense pre-war world
They backdate their wedding for shame
of a child born too soon
All she remembers is Conrad's *Typhoon*
on a listing London stage

The Fernery...1923

Light meanders through stained glass
seeks out the moist mating of moss and fern
The serious girl in tiered satin and lace
stands by her younger brother who grows up
to become a doctor despite or because
of a collarbone set without expert help
She coaches him, waves him to war
nurses her ailing mother
banishes her own medical ambitions

The Conferring…1933

Muted sound and light reflect
from the polished wood of fluted ceilings
The serious woman in gown and mortarboard
embarks on a teaching career but
is forced to resign on marriage
Spends years proving her domestic talents
to her man's mother and sisters
and raising four children
while her sharp brain scrambles

Stillborn

Four children later
her grief buried deep
in an unmarked grave
she still wishes she had
seen his strangely large feet
touched his waxed monkey face
circled her warmth round his cooling skin
known more than the name she gave him
in a sleepwalking dream

Comet

My mother was born in 1910
Halley's Comet made her welcome

in its elliptical way, then trailing
its tail of dirty snowballs left
to brighten the nooks
of the solar system, while she

navigated around the black holes
of two world wars which sucked in
men, materials, whole landscapes
and the light of human kindness

Deaths of parents, brothers, husband, child
a backdrop of dark matter
TB and polio flared briefly then burned out
like meteors entering earth's atmosphere

Cars and planes criss-crossed the planet
in ever more frenetic schedules
Radio, phone and TV waves jostled
for space with the twinkling of stars

Love pulsed like the red spot on Jupiter
the moon's cycle gave her hope of renewal
and on cloudless nights the Milky Way
shone lambently upon her

My mother died in 1986
Halley's Comet bade her farewell

In the year of my birth

February 1942

Out of a grey cyclonic sky
Japanese bombers in close formation
like eagles trained into social groups
like wasps even less social than usual
like everything you thought you'd never
see or want to see, swoop on Darwin
shocking waves through tropical air
scooping the sea into white-maned cavalry

Waves of anxiety break over Melbourne
engulf my mother's body, the rapid beat
of her heart hastening my own

I respond with frenzy
kicking waves to keep at bay
a world I'm afraid to enter
It is written that war babies
are born anxious and stay that way

July 1942

My father builds an air raid shelter
under the pear tree
my mother draws the blackout curtains

The North African sirocco blows
Rommel towards Montgomery
whips the sand into bayonet points
sends hot news of an allied victory
across the Mediterranean
to reverberate in cold southern climes
of a planet spinning out of kilter

I'm twisted into pretzel shapes
as I navigate the birth canal
emerging like a red lizard
sounding like a wild cat

The Annual Sunday School Picnic at Hanging Rock

Cup day. Melbourne gallops
from spring's pastel tones
to the bold voice of summer

All aboard the square bottle-green bus
sing along to Dad's mouth organ
as we ride across the volcanic plain

We've come to this old race-track
to be distracted by our elders
from the holiday debauchery of the city

The rock hangs out
haunted by a hanged bushranger
where gas bubbled up through lava

like the effervescence of adolescence
Gas tickles my nose from the lemonade
masquerading as Flemington bubbly

Far from the hurry of hooves
we stake our all on races in sacks
three-legged or egg-and-spoon

It's years before Joan Lindsay's book
but something holds us down below, cloistered
with sandwiches, rosellas and small victories

Man Playing Harmonica

After the Welsh concert I'm marching
to 'Men of Harlech'
On Princes Bridge I pass an old man

a box of coins at his side
Just as my father did, he plays a harmonica
one hand cupped over the end

'Royal Telephone', the song
my father asked for on his deathbed
jangles over the pavement

I throw gold into the battered box
wanting to thank him
for something I can't put into words

Cruise boats flatten under bridges
twilight runners are intent
on their own heartbeats

The Yarra glides on, dividing the city
I watch the carriage lamps reflected in the water
as the old man plays 'Moon River'

Wrist Bones

As my father grew older, felt his sap
and his belly thickening, he would bring
to the table a small jar of bones

chunky, in liquid
two bones, greenish, furred
impossibly fractured

dancing on the current a slow *pas de deux*
Both deceptively large in refracted light
one sometimes hiding the other

These were the bones that had stopped him
balancing, twisting, supporting himself
on parallel bars or painting sought-after oils

but couldn't stop him
conjuring trinkets from our ears
with a flick of his wrist

The four of us

seem strangely large
strung across the footpath
like warning signs in this doll's village
where midget memories sidle by
hugging the fence line

We've paused in picking over the old home
found yellowed satin shoes   an old mincer
a poison pen letter   Fourteen van loads
consigned to the tip to be picked over
by seagulls

From interiors airbrushed by our father
in pale rainbow colours
we've emerged into a June landscape
of faded Arkley exteriors cowering
behind high cypress hedges

Three brothers and a sister
bound together by ghostly shackles
we amble to lunch at shops spawned
like garish toadstools from the rich
humus of their ancestors

Conversation skims lightly
over quicksands then back to salvage duty
Like Alice on drinking the magic potion
our elbows and knees keep blocking
the cupboards and corners

Travelling Companion

You step out into my horror zone
my heart in your parachute pack
Taut sinews
        jolt wings of silk
mushrooming into gentleness
I stitch a skin of wind
to a cloud and hawk-like
fix you with my sextant eye
to set you down
        in wild sweet grass

You ski down wedding-cake slopes
smoothed strange by winter's knife
Thighs scream
        ankles answer
and when white-out spins
your degrees of freedom
follow my spoor to the snow-fox lair
My soft pelt will warm you
my sixth sense
        will guide you home

Scuba tanks full you fall
overboard backwards as though
embellishing
      some drunken party
Even sharks are afraid of this
crazy cross between lungfish
and alien eel bifurcated in black
and yellow.
But I know the trouble
you have with bubbles and nudge you
breath wise
      up water to sky

Taking Tea

'Humanity has met in a teacup' – Okakura Kakuzo

Wading through honeyed air
to a lemon-lit room
I find you pouring tea
jasmine scenting your hair

Silver bamboo bones
frame ink on silk
A bird with jade eyes
hovers over water

Around secret spaces my words
curl green-tipped tongues
which you wrap in muslin
to blunt the points of pain

In white porcelain cups
you brew an elixir
from my dross
We drink as one

Elemental

1 Fire

Draggled to birth
fireball at sputter speed

Dark matter muscles
your tight cap of flame

The cord pays out
a slow-burning wick

keeps you in revolution
too close   too far

I lie gutted
like a spent candle

2 Earth

Your earth pivots
       on this moment
tilting into seasons

where strings dance puppets
       down chasms
and monkeys stay tethered to tunes

Trails dead-end
       and double-back
clogging your socks with burrs

sleepers woken by bells
       startle upright
track straight to nowhere

3 Air

All strings attached
        cord rips   you float
harnessed by clouds
        in carnival shapes

home-in on a dew-lit runway
        walk a spider's slackrope
stepwise polygons framing
        the centre of solitary predation

when all you wanted
        was to lasso a star
and ride it through
        applauding night

4 Water

You shoot through tea tree
nuzzle wet sand   fizzle

heavy-handed undertow
sinks your compass

memories dissolve into
thickening blood

A teasing net woven
from strands of your life

bundles glazed bodies
tipping the scales with gold

Snow Gum

On your birthday I'm alone in a crowd
of snow gums
Down the trunk of the nearest tree
grey and green saunter companionably
Ochre ribbons narrow to scarlet claws
The Kimberley has come to the High Country

Rippled bark outstrips the wood
A knot resembles a head hidden
in a child's puzzle
a swatch of twigs a winged eyebrow
the eye a wad of sap
a red crescent the lower lid

The trunk sports peaks and gullies
microcosms carolled by currawongs
in cradles of snow
An aura of sound envelops me
as I relive the colours
of your birth

Span

His hand is a butterfly drying its wings
a starburst   a starfish groping
a hand wise and water-beaten
lines silver-crossing and illegible
the lifeline interrupted as if by pulsing waves

He clasps her lifebuoy finger
she strokes his skin   electric shock
of silk on ivory   knucklebones waiting
for the toss

his skull a phrenology
of threat and promise

The tea leaves in her cup scatter
a road vanishing to infinity

She stares into the crystal balls
of his eyes hazel swirling around
the pupils reflecting only herself

When he hugs her so tight
she can hardly breathe
she reads the long bones
the soft cartilage end zones
ossifying with chilling finality

Digging

Fate dragged me across the continent
to give birth amongst kind faces
of strangers in a city springing from desert

We haven't been back in thirty years
to revisit the house where our son rode
the merry-go-round of his infancy

toughening his feet on hot pavements
digging memories into sandy soil
Nothing is familiar now

We dine in a wild park overlooking the city
New buildings sparkle and the river slithers
like a jewelled snake

All those years ago we celebrated here
with trepidation
the news of his beginning

And we were right to be afraid
like diggers venturing hundreds of miles
through wilderness to return years later

unbearably aged
with callused feet
and a few specks of gold

My Poem

begins as a cake of soap
rectangular and suggestible
that virgin smell tinged
with the indefinable
lavender   eucalyptus   carbolic

My knife scrapes and slithers
a primitive profile
a face squashed against glass
Fathoming the lode
I gouge out an ear
sharpen a nose
repair a drooping eye

Warm tears blur the vision
until my poem fits
the hollow of my hand

On the balcony

Paired cumquat trees
        in sage tubs
distinguish this balcony
        which is hers
but not hers   The hot night
will not relinquish it

Wind waves over her
        then retreats
dumping a flotsam of soot
and torn petals

Garlic voices levitate
        through lemongrass
rank with smog and rotten egg
        Inside the room music
beats the air   mixes it
with mothballs and lavender

In this liminal zone
        she can make
no decisions
They are made for her

Her beauty ebbs
        to its passionate core
her body takes any shape
        the night embraces
her child blows away in a gale
her job follows

A stream of thresholds in time
        and space
                opens before her

Immortality

It's something you want a bit or a lot
and you'll work, in proportion, to reach it
with diets and dyes, gymnastics and creams
and anything else you can think of

Becoming a god or goddess would do
or perhaps an elf or a gnome
may grant your wish for eternal life
if your youth can go on and on

Your children will carry your qualities forward
enhanced, suppressed or denied
known only as long as your grandchildren live
or as long as your memories survive

In a world quickly warming, freezing's a counter
to hotted-up, ageing you
but you live beyond your use-by date
and you'll thaw to torpid stew

Cloning's a trick for identical you
and would keep you on track for a while
until old cells in young flesh grow weary and stiff
Too soon you become senile

Back in the fifties a biopsy performed
on the cervix of 'Helen Lane'
cultured cells which divided in chaos and haste
and have done so again and again

How strange to imagine a piece of yourself
lasting not only so long
but propagated around the world
in the labs of the youthful and strong

Transience

The boundary thrums
Cars jostling for tyrehold
disgorge small boys
in shorts and lurid jumpers
Scarcely room for my bike to pass

My eyes zoom in on the scrum
        bounce/kick
        knock/scurry
        grab/swing
knees green and muddy

One boy, stocky and red-haired
reminds me of my long gone son
taking a punt on slush, jabbing
opponents, handballing advice
a crescendo of throwaway lines

My eyes pan to the frosted fringes
where scarfed mothers nurse babies
and coffee and fathers
strut their former glory
I envy their carefree talk

Wild fowl squawk
from nearby wetlands
where serried ranks of foxtails
decimated by drought
sway to the barracking

When I ride back
two hours later, the team
with all its baggage
has gone like Brigadoon
the field wreathed in mist

Looking Back

Feet pounding, pausing
slipping off the shoulder
to the paddock where horses graze

Ahead, a gravelled track
an ancient red gum, limbs gnarled
some amputated to roundness
twisted by erratic weather
wisdom deep beneath the bark

I salute the sun
pluck a pocketful of cumulus
A cloud of thrips patters my face
streams away behind me
I don't know how I've reached this point
but sense how far I've come

into enfolding silence
By the warning of carrot bait
a young rabbit skips across the track
The conjunction of youth and death
trips latent memories

Looking back I see you sleeping
your long lashes the envy of any girl
I touch your skin, feel the tingle
earthing me and like Eurydice
you die to me again

I would rather be Lot's wife
a pillar of salt to be licked by horses
their long-lashed eyes closing in ecstasy
as yours did, at my breast

Plenty River Trail

Last rays squint down the valley
where traffic-light rosellas
harry the leaf litter crawlers
Sweet vegetable smells dance
around dark-sharpened eyes
A white scut signals from the roots
of a swaggering red gum
Kookaburras vie for encores

A kangaroo, ears at the ready, bounds
the fence and vanishes in tall grass
because a girl, carrot in hand, mother in tow
runs down the path to the horse, strokes
his sleek head with peerless joy and when
the crunch comes, surrenders

Haiku

Midnight branches
a possum
walks over the moon

        Pollen sprays my window
        graffiti of spring

leaf suspended
from spider web
silent wind-chimes

        Jostling for sunlight
        with overgrown apple boughs
        a single red rose

fading sunlight horses crop the horizon

City Park

By day, home to saunterers
seizing every bench in the shade
except this one under the oldest elm

A new walker stumbles
into his mother's approval

seagulls strut and squawk down rivals
government grinds on behind elegant facades

Everywhere noise is marginalised

I feel the gnarl of roots
sense them questing beneath me
at the slow urge of water

This space bides its time

At nightfall the smell of decay
rises on warm air and the truce
is broken

Polished metal banding trunks
thwarts possums
Claws slide and screech
like fingernails on blackboards

The message is clear

Luna Park

After Soul Singer at Luna Park, Perceval

Enter grinning moon mouth
crowds of donut mouths
and fairy floss fingers

Accordion Man all mouth
and rubber fingers

plays Big Dipper
manhole mouths
scream out hearts
fingers steel on steel

sings Ghost Train
white-knuckle fingers
jam blue-rimmed mouths

Gravitron guts
fill gravel mouths
spider fingers
glued to wall

Accordion Man all fingers
and rubber mouth
sings his soul

Angel on Swanston

White
from sleek hair to slippers
she pirouettes powdered skin
Clockwork wave
        eyes on blue alert
Kerbside
        gilt coach and placid pair

At joyful news I've sometimes seen
a white wingtip vanish into shadow
or at a loved one's death
a black feather float
        from somewhere secret
A presence in corners
        on shoulders

But never until now
halo at her feet
to gather gold

Josephine Bonaparte at Malmaison

A cure for a sick house in a sick country
is a garden throbbing with exotic life
I have brought the Antipodes to Paris
to heal and intrigue, to take my mind
off the sharpness of death

Kangaroos abound, their deer-like heads
cresting the foliage and cockatoos
flaunting golden crowns screech
to a halt on eucalypt boughs
Water moles burrow in secret mud

The swans are black as the natives
of *Terres Australes* or the trunks
of fire-ravaged forests
Some expect them to moult
to their natural white

Mimosa and boronia mimic sun and stars
hark back to my tropical childhood
They thrive in the hothouse like embryos
in the fecund womb I would love to possess
If only Napoleon could reproduce

by bud, cutting or runner
With gentle secateurs I dead-head the roses
This pink and cream with foxed petals
reminds me so much of my first husband
beheaded in full flower by his country

Marie Curie

Roughshod hooves bruise flesh, smash bone
a wild, wet night of mud and gore
Her life contracts, goes on alone

Stumbling, distracted, umbrella blown
wheels grind on; he hears no more
Roughshod hooves bruise flesh, smash bone

In a shed as cold as they'd ever known
together they shovelled the dull brown ore
Her life contracts, goes on alone

Patients were dying, queues had grown
always more pitchblende heaped on the floor
Roughshod hooves bruise flesh, smash bone

A faint blue glow from the stubborn stone
the ramparts breached in a silent war
Her life contracts, goes on alone

Hands scarred, eyes blurred, the die is thrown
The healing rays leave body raw
Roughshod hooves bruise flesh, smash bone
Her life contracts, goes on alone

Einstein's Wife

From letters between Mileva Maric and Albert Einstein

You asked me not to write to you until
boredom became my constant companion
and now I pace lock step with it under
the German oaks of our tranquil Neckar valley
I'm as restless as the babe in my womb

The fog is lonely as infinity and yet
my happiness would be infinite
if only you were here
you who understands infinity of space
but cannot fathom my corner of it

The sour cherry trees bloom
for the second time this year
In the soft spring sunshine
I crave a copy of the Helmholtz
Wave Theory of Light

Consider the Law of Molecular Forces
galvanise your rigid body
with a sinusoidal current and come to me
before the kisses I have saved
overflow their bowl and vanish

Neptune's Wife

She is immortal woman
        Dark currents of hair
        skin creamy as cloud
in silhouette through mist and fog
Sending the ocean out for the long haul
she watches the slow glide of sunset

Past has no meaning
present and future are one
        She collects leftover dreams
        warms them up   to feed her yearning
Has long since grown a shell around
her soft body of sorrow

Immunised by fear her blood
readies for attack
        She knows the cruelty
        and beneficence of water
communes with fish and crab
the ebb and flow of seabirds

Spontaneous Generation

1 Bruises

Blossoming all over my body
purple pansies complete
with yellow centres

their origins lost
in a hotchpotch
of invisible corners

As the moon softly segues
new bruises follow old
a trail of dying blood

2 Millipedes

High on white walls
they appear
as if by sleight of hand
Comma-shaped
they punctuate my reverie

coiling tightly when touched
like ammonites found fossilised
in limestone cliffs

Flushed down drains
they crawl back on myriad legs
and hide from dusters
long enough
to crumble into oblivion

3 Mushrooms

An under-wired network of spies
hooded and vulnerable bursts
overnight through yesterday's pristine lawn

Their earthiness speaks to palate
and nose of underworld riches
forbidden succulence

Hyenas of the plant kingdom
they feed on broken bodies
rejigging fern and flower

into dwarf parasols whose spokes
fling millions of spores
to scavenge the world

Upstarts growing tall on manure
voracious as caterpillars
ephemeral as butterflies

To make bread

I sift flour into a warm basin

My fingers drip silken gloves
        then scoop a hollow
                for yeast
crumbled from its sloth

Imbibing nectar it buds
        microscopic chaos
Bubbles celebrate renewal

Stern salt sprinkled at the edges
        cannot spike
the jubilation

I knead the dough into compliance
        fingers coaxing
                knuckles punishing
until heat smooths the evidence

bakes a holey sacrifice

Breakthrough

At the heart of the garden
concrete is bone deep
        marked out in squares

Swept and weeded it draws
smug looks from the tenant
        who fails to notice

wind and rain feathering
earth around the edges
        mossing the grooves

Leaves hide the drain   suckers
smother light and violets
        are the new wallflowers

Steam-puffs from the pool
coax geraniums to
        break cover

A wattle strains its roots
and a jagged crack
        widens to a grin

Crane

I try to see the crane

> ringed by fire-glo
> witches' hats
> diverting the traffic
> to querulous queues
> latticed neck
> swinging rigidly
> past blank windows
> guzzling rubble
> squat body roaring

as a member of genus Grus

> lately arrived from Siberia
> on icy currents of air
> dancing between lily pads
> long neck swivel-
> ling its bill
> tweezing morsels
> of pond life
> its cry muted
> by a tangle of weeds

but fail utterly

Flamingo

Can't imagine a flamingo
doing the flamenco
but it does
its shrimp-pink version of a flame

dancing a minuet
across stagnant water
its head upside-down
submerged

blue whale of birds
beak curved and toothed
sieving food
from the water

giraffe of birds
knock-kneed on land
symphonic in air
neck and legs stretched

the winding skein of wings
slowly beating
its airy bones riding the currents
south to Africa

Flapper

After the painting by Margaret Preston

At first gaze, steady   mutual
nothing flighty about her
except knees   crossed and
exposed by the checked dress
       with Peter Pan collar

But ending my scan
at the small-brimmed
safe for church hat hiding
cropped hair and eyebrows
       (plucked perhaps)

I notice the feathers, sleek   alert
Like the wild duckling she waits
poised for take off   Away from
the languor of boudoir and parlour
to a world where the air pulsates

Haiku

crumbs and conversation
sparrows hop into coffee shop

                    wattlebird trapped by its image
                    one tap on the glass sets it free

river in flood
among scotch thistles
a patch of pink lilies

                    Sipping nectar
                    outside the café window
                    yellow-bellied sunbird

blackbird's orange beak opens the morning

White Bees

On the pilgrimage of the Camino de Santiago de Compostela, Northern Spain

In Melbourne's winter as I prepared
for my pilgrimage, magnolia buds burst
Bees bustled between pink camellias
embroidering a grey sky
a dash of galah colours to lift the spirits

Now we pilgrims scorch along the trail
through pine and oak
drink sangria and beer
pray by the tomb of San Juan
keeper of the unborn souls of children

Legend has it
that when the tomb opens
these souls
embodied in white bees
swarm out floating like a bridal veil

A sleeping woman, still young but barren
feels the tickle of tiny feet
the whir of diaphanous wings
the sting
as the infant soul enters her womb

A tale of divine conception
to rival the Christ child's
Sanctifying the weary pilgrimage
No stranger than cabbage patch
stork and cradle ship

Cathedral

Locks and bolts are all about
stopping angels creeping through
as well as many a local lout

whose spray-paint drips from wall to pew
like umbrellas not quite dry
and black as any witches brew

ominous as winter sky
while down below around the font
newts and toads prepare to die

a sacrifice as is their wont
to make the best communion wine
despite the smell that says they don't

Altar saints in states divine
carved in wood from elm and oak
come to life and join the line

with sinners and some unknown folk
who wish to dip or drink or both
to pledge themselves in sacred yoke

While decked in ash and mourning cloth
they celebrate the Devil's wrath

Wasp Attack

As colour leaves the trees
and returns to the lawn
wasps circle, nonchalant
waiting for traffic to clear
from the bunker
in the stump's soft centre

I stoop to sabotage the nest
At the rearguard blitz I stagger back
in frenzied batting at wasps
tangling my hair, clothes-crawling
stinging me over and under

At dusk when the wasps have clocked in
I don battle gear and spray revenge
in dense white powder

The garden is mine again

Heat Wave

Waves of heat ripple
through spaced-out air
The elderly gasp like landed fish

People stroll in shopping mall cool
while their countless cars
roast on concrete

Chocolate swoons
over parboiled lemons
straight from the tree

Like a buckled rail track
a trail of ants winds from
nowhere on its journey to water

Cockroaches breach the kitchen
I answer the door to the frenzied
buzzing of flies

The mirror, always unstable
loses a leg when the glue melts
Shatters

Adds to the gloom
of long-range forecasts
worse than any yet recorded

A stunned bird falls into
the mouth of a languid cat
Straw lawns crunch underfoot

Ground cover rolls
green leaves into grey scrolls
bearing only bad news

Trees bake and burn
in this oven set on high
Fall into an early autumn

Arsonists smudge charcoal over
the land, survey their handiwork
with furtive satisfaction

Coolers roar like landing aircraft
Europe freezes in the coldest
pinch for years

Bushfire

Morning
        I open my door
to the smell of burning

Smoke screens the distance
khaki paddocks cropped
down to grassroots

The wind turns
butterflies scorch into houses
gather in low corners

Fire-giants fierce
as five hundred Hiroshimas
darken the skies

tremble the hills
eat towns encroaching on bush
leave nothing to sift from the ash

save a chrysalis of hope
Remnant trees stand
like exclamation marks

Evening
        the sun an eye
reddened by smoke and tears

Burning

Bark dry with drought
and shedding

shreds curled in secret scrolls
ready to catch as flames

hatch from bellowed sparks
burn down layers

cleansing   destroying
Charred vessels leak

precious fluids like time
through wormholes

Deep-down buds waken
penetrate ash

reach for stars burning
histories into life

Waking

From dreams of boneless fish adorned
with thornless roses I wade into the morning
Calendar leaves fall and the January
        I once knew is gone

Blindly I feel your face
the way you keep silent
speaks volumes   I must know
if the pain describes
        the wound

Standing outside myself I see my body
as an aerial map   hills   fern gullies
flowing scars   Each part has different
memories and would weep
        if it could

In the backyard of life an old man pegs
rags to an antique chair   Death forewarns
with home-delivered groceries
Lesser mortals pass the baton
        to eccentricity

Sometimes I fall down the well
of remembering how quickly we forget
Stepping off the treadmill my body feels
        light as air

Waiting for the light

Until the earth and I roll over
I believe this blackness is death

(bird cacophony the argument of angels
the possum on the roof Thanatos
come to collect me)

the warm death of skin-to-skin correspondence
of bears hibernating in forest caves
the smell of honey tasted with furred tongue

I dream of a jester with mismatched body parts
juggling pain and pleasure in random assortment

until a chink of light spreads down the long
white tunnel through which I may return

Book Launch

En route to the book launch
I step down to the toilet snuggled
in the crook of the Town Hall's elbow

In floral jeans and jacket, a woman
prone on the tiled floor, head pillowed
on knapsack, reminds me of Ophelia

water withheld in cisterns and bowls
She seems deeply asleep
but could be drugged or dead

No one touches her porcelain
skin for fear of needle-stick
or wake-in-fright

We step over her body
wash our hands of her
with stubs of well-used soap

On to the launch, spruikers dizzy
with spin, piles of hardbacks
slippery with gloss

The erstwhile politician bragging
in plummy tones and 'passing'
on difficult questions, has written

his government into folk lore
Audience outrage stifles
the lone protester

We file out for buying and signing
Two policemen in rubber gloves
step down to the Town Hall toilet

Lake Bonney

The lake lies in wait
for water
The trees are destitute
and the grey patina of death

spreads over split branches
pointing askew as if in accusation
the only sign of health the pink blush
on evening's cheek

White men dug deep to build a bridge
their muscles wriggling like ferrets
sweat splashing on black men's bones
unearthed and fractured again

They built these bones into the struts
and spans of the bridge
finger bones pointing
thumb bones caught mid-twiddle

foot bones splayed from too much walking
leg bones bowed from a weight too great to bear
Bones augmented and cemented
Black and white lives bridging the gap

Cast

Holocaust memorial, Budapest

Metal shoes wait
in a higgledy row
on the bank of the Danube

Cast in iron
from leather shoes
flogged within an inch
of muddy lives

They placed their shoes
beside folded jackets
then were shot
and cast into brown waters

I feel the warmth
of the summer sun
inside each shoe
the warmth of each foot

Coast

Marram grass sends runners
announcing its clawback
to drought-bitten loam
Aching for equilibrium
I tread the grass down
to high-water line

Crabs transparent as desire
career sideways   dig in
to burst further on
through a tumour of sand

A gull riding the waves
its featherweight balanced
by upthrusting sea
dives for a fish swimming
out of its depth

A kite hovers
then dips to the tug
of some invisible hand

A Visit to the Aquarium

I'm in the city with a ticket to the aquarium

Rain nails its credentials to the roofs
splurging its gurgles on gutters and gardens
Conversation ripples through currents of traffic
Dolphin music calms the rudderless crowd

Little Bourke for lunch
in a goldfish bowl café
I'm staring into a tank of jittery crabs
their claws lashed together

Shark's fin soup is on the menu
The waiter, a gelled fin
cresting his scalp
undulates between tables

Waves of shoppers surge from a nearby store
A stingray of a man flaps his long grey coat
around a huddle of women
parcels grasped with octopus strength

A man surfs from the Yarra Hotel
the street swimming before his eyes
The doorman in penguin suit
looks down his beaklike nose

I don't need that ticket to the aquarium

Perspective

after *Frank's Dam and Jet* 2002 oil on linen by Michael Kelly

1

From where I stand the dam stretches
its broad face half given to reflection
Banks startled by exposure
wear a sparse cover of tufts

Smudged trees circling the hill
shade its imperfections
and give the grass
a new lease of green

The jet taking you from me
is a silver cross punched out of cloud
an insect vulnerable but uncaring
as it makes a beeline for home

2

From where I sit over the wing
sharp peaks edge out the forest
skirt memories of you
Cottonwool clouds soak up the sun

scud by intent
on losing me in blue infinity
and weather your choice of paradise
The dam winks from a small corner

of brown-green patchwork
where you are absorbed
into the water, the soil, the trees
I could not persuade you to leave

Leaving

New pink leaves shiny with spring tremble
in the breeze of first argument
He refuses to mow the lawn
she won't hire a man to do it
The cats swivel their ears
and cultivate the neighbours

A north wind gathering grievances
rattles restraint
Where do his kids sleep when they visit?
Her kids are greedy for bed room
and can't bear to share

One year later, a hurricane sweeps
up the scraps of discord
and hammers their union
She spends her wage at the pokies
He earns scarcely enough
for the food she refuses to cook

We watch him loading the trailer
with the treadmill, the punching bag
and the fishing line he had no time to cast
He's leaving in a tail wind
his red-haired son gravely smiling

Pluto to Proserpina

News report: The world's oldest face cream has been found in a drain at a Roman temple site in London.

This offering from the overworld puzzles me
for here there are no wrinkles but skin
cupid-fine as yours suffers where plants
grow pale and tall searching
      for the hint of light

I will smooth your body with the magic
we gods let men discover and have
ourselves forgotten   You are my bedrock
for all growing things and cracks
      must be repaired

You are the fire at my core
Your skin blazes to be soothed
Without you I freeze like the iceberg
whose haunch you caress
      with a cheek burnt cold

Your mask is the cave's mystery weaving
round stalagmites on steps lit
by glow-worms   And somewhere out of time
your supplicants will know
      they pleased you

Underground car park at dawn

After *Adelaide* 1983, a pencil drawing by Janenne Eaton

Sunlight is forbidden
its relentless way
of holding up to scorn
Down here it's deliciously cold
all sharpness and angles
like a smart black hat tilted rakishly
shadows hunched in corners
echoes of footsteps disembodied

miasmas of oil and exhaust
white-ant the foundations
of the city
All is order and solitude
in tune with the deep past
nearer the centre of things

Burke longs for Julia

Burke and Wills expedition (1860–61)

My fingers enter your glove's suppleness
white kid caressing my skin
smoothing your soul into mine
Broad knuckles meet with soft rebuff

I cannot reach those sweet cul-de-sacs
cannot mould myself to you
until journey's end yokes
your faith to my love

Which casket shall I open?
Mountains tormented by monsoons
my strength half-drowned
in the surge of a creek
I have named after you

or the dingo's lament
across flatness of desert
whipped clean by the wind
and despair burnt into my brain

With my dream on its knees
to the song you are singing
and no flesh left to cushion my bones
my fingers dissolve into yours

Aboard The Lady Jocelyn

Plymouth to Melbourne, 1869–70

Woken at six by timber bones plangent
under torture and the far off rumbling
of a wave gathering leviathan strength

My Irish babes born too soon
frail and pellucid as shrimps
mew faintly like distant sea birds

That wave hunched over splinters
the cabin and shudders my heart
My twins lie still and blue in their crib

My prayers ripped by the wind
small bodies sewn into sailcloth
slip over the side

Two flying fish in our wake

The Rajah Quilt

Sewn by convict women aboard the *Rajah*, 1841

Truly this ship is a seahorse
bucking and straining
Again I prick my finger
blood speckling the appliquéd flowers

So dim below decks
and we Pentonville women so weak
only porridge in our bellies
we sometimes sew patches back to front

One hundred days from Woolwich
five from Van Diemen's Land
We've nearly finished our task
just enough silk to embroider

the inscription to the ladies
of the Convict Ship Committee
who farewelled us with hessian bags
of needles, thread and scraps

Make something of yourselves
Make something for posterity
Some of us, old hands at needlecraft
help others to inch the cloth

a chessboard of textures
something solid to hang on to
in this lonely turmoil
of sky and sea

Our teacher has caught the eye
of the captain but we drabs can only
stitch our hope and our sorrow into this quilt
and know not whose bed it will cover

Lady of Sandstone

Sydney

From higgledy streets
flanked by sandstone grandeur
I'm ascending steps

hemmed in by her rock walls
squashed into nightmare spaces
of convict ships and prison cells

Always upward
the breathlessness of perpetual
climbing to breathtaking views

overlooking the adamantine
winking of water in cahoots
with sand drifting down

to make more stone
like the spine of mountains
at my back

Released from one
confinement to another
on the biggest island in the world

Lady of Limestone

Adelaide

City of Light, surrounded by vineyards
haven from persecution
her land uplifted from sea
an ancient graveyard of shells and bones

Her water, too limey to lather
drips from the roofs of caves
sculpting shapes too grim
for the sun to contemplate

young men drowned in the Torrens
bodies in barrels
murdered girls
missing children

all hidden by a genteel veneer
Founded by jailbirds
and named for a queen
she is corseted between hills and coast

can only expand north and south
into pockets of poverty
where the thin green line
beats back the desert

Lady of Bluestone

Melbourne

She blocked out gutters
raised gaols, cathedrals, barracks
A sober city of landed gentry drunk on gold
Crinolines on convict foundations

Caught in cross currents
at the continent's corner
a character quirky and unformed
from the pages of a Dickens novel

Now trams belt out their rackety rhythm
and the Yarra, boasting a novel purity
jams traffic across scarce bridges
where cruise boats do the limbo

Like some benign growth
she spreads lopsidedly around the bay
keeping her distance from the ancient
volcanic plain out west

I know her as my birth mother
Our souls have merged
clouding my judgement
of her faults and foibles

Writers' Block

Drought sets me thinking of deserts
where camels muse   faces shifty
as sand dunes   knees worn out
like magic carpets on fancy flights

Cactus takes a stab
red splurge of single flower
With luck I'll find a bloated frog
dug in below the claypan

In the suburbs maple too frugal
to sprout misses out on autumn
stretches roots   nobbles the lawn
and taps the water table

Red topped and tailed finches
springboard from grass stalks
to poetry when wetlands once again
can claim the name

Soliloquy

Meditation queues grow longer
the swing door ushers us in/out
time fixes the ice man wood man
bread man in aspic or amber
snakes appear across our paths
do we swerve or break their backs
dip inside the body for equations
that solve riddles

glacial calm follows the smashing
of doors keys never fit
life is lived in the interstices
where mint flourishes its scent
like cheap chocolate
we have brittle shells/soft centres

www.ingramcontent.com/pod-product-compliance
Lightning Source LLC
Chambersburg PA
CBHW070049120526
44589CB00034B/1679